EARTH'S HOTTEST PLACE

and Other Earth Science Records

by Martha E. H. Rustad

Consulting Editor: Gail Saunders-Smith, PhD

CAPSTONE PRESS
a capstone imprint

Pebble Plus is published by Capstone Press,
1710 Roe Crest Drive, North Mankato, Minnesota 56003
www.capstonepub.com

Library of Congress Cataloging-in-Publication Data
Cataloging-in-Publication information is on file with the Library of Congress.
ISBN 978-1-4765-0257-1 (library binding)
ISBN 978-1-4765-3474-9 (ebook PDF)

Editorial Credits
Erika L. Shores, editor; Lori Bye, designer; Eric Gohl, media researcher; Jennifer Walker, production specialist

Photo Credits
Alamy: The Natural History Museum, 13; Corbis: Louie Psihoyos, 15, Visuals Unlimited/Tim Hauf, 11; Dreamstime: Shantel Adolpho, 19; Getty Images: National Geographic/Carsten Peter, 17; NASA: 21; Shutterstock: Damian Gil, 9, James Mattil, 5, Redshinestudio (grunge border), throughout, Tomaj Szymanski, cover, Volodymyr Goinyk, 7

Note to Parents and Teachers

The Wow! set supports national science standards related to earth science. This book describes and illustrates record-breaking earth science facts. The images support early readers in understanding the text. The repetition of words and phrases helps early readers learn new words. This book also introduces early readers to subject-specific vocabulary words, which are defined in the Glossary section. Early readers may need assistance to read some words and to use the Table of Contents, Glossary, Read More, Internet Sites, and Index sections of the book.

Printed in the United States of America in North Mankato, Minnesota.
032013   007223CGF13

TABLE OF CONTENTS

WEATHER

Records are set every day in earth science. California's Death Valley hit 134 degrees Fahrenheit (56.7°Celsius) on July 10, 1913. No place has ever been hotter.

Antarctica is Earth's coldest place. July 21, 1983, dropped to a record -128°F (-89°C). At that temperature, skin and everything else freezes in seconds.

The Atacama Desert in Chile is

one of the driest places on Earth.

Some spots in the desert went

400 years without rain.

ON THE EARTH

Wham! A meteorite smashed into

South Africa 2 billion years ago.

It made Earth's biggest crater.

It's 99 miles (159 kilometers) wide.

IN THE EARTH

Could you hold 157 pounds

(71 kilograms) of gold?

In 1869 miners dug up

a nugget that size in Australia.

Canada's Dinosaur Provincial Park holds the most kinds of dinosaur fossils. Scientists know that at least 35 kinds of dinosaurs once lived there.

15

You'll find the world's biggest cave in a jungle in Vietnam. Son Doong cave is at least 3 miles (4.8 km) long.

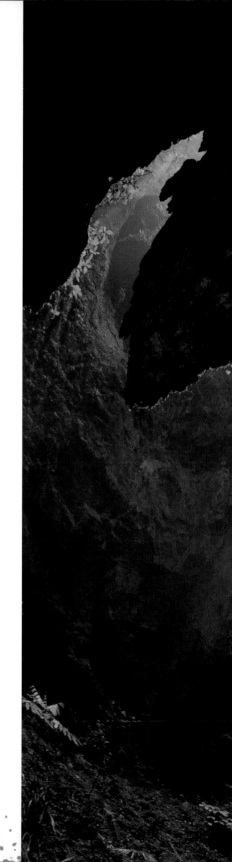

VOLCANOES

Hawaii's Mauna Loa is the world's biggest volcano. It towers 13,677 feet (4,169 meters) above sea level. Lava last blasted from it in 1984.

Mauna Loa

In 2011 an underwater volcano erupted in the Red Sea. Lava hardened and formed the world's newest island.

lava—hot, liquid rock that pours out of a volcano when it erupts

meteorite—a piece of rock from space that strikes a planet or a moon

nugget—a lump of gold or other metal found in the earth

record—when something is done better than anyone or anything has ever done it before

volcano—a mountain that sometimes sends out hot lava, steam, and ash

READ MORE

Peppas, Lynn. *The Atacama Desert.* Deserts around the World. New York: Crabtree Pub. Co., 2013.

Schuh, Mari. *Volcanoes.* Earth in Action. Mankato, Minn.: Capstone Press, 2010.

Simon, Seymour. *Seymour Simon's Extreme Earth Records.* San Francisco: Chronicle Books, 2012.

INTERNET SITES

FactHound offers a safe, fun way to find Internet sites related to this book. All of the sites on FactHound have been researched by our staff.

Here's all you do:

Visit *www.facthound.com*

Type in this code: 9781476502571

Super-cool stuff! Check out projects, games and lots more at www.capstonekids.com

23

INDEX

Word Count: 202
Grade: 1
Early-Intervention Level: 18